The

SPEAKER'S TOOLBOX

For

Professional Storytellers

Be a Better Storyteller with Powerful Tools

Over 103 tools to add to your Toolbox for success

By **Tom Hobbs**

"Most excellent story tellers have failed when they went to the professional stage."

- T. George, "Uncle Tom"

The tools in this book will help you be the valued presenter that should be paid well for your craft. If you are presenting a Story, a workshop or coordinating a big event this book is for you. From small story circles to an auditorium a professional will be appreciated and referred for more gigs. Many of these tools are similar for every presenter that works professionally. You are worthy of being the Master of Storytelling   not the amateur of tales.

Your words and ideas matter. Share them professionally.

Cheers,
Tom
The Man In The Hat

The Speaker's Toolbox by Tom G. Hobbs
Copyright © 2014

Content first published in White Pages 2012, 2013

Table of Contents

Acknowledgements

I give 703 gallons of "Thanks" to Joe Sabah. The man who continues to give me and thousands of others a gentle push with his thumb in our back to go speak to the world.

He is a mentor to the world of Professional Speakers.

Cheers
Tom Hobbs
The Man In The Hat

Why this book?

After attending 100's of speaking events I found many successful ways to be a better speaker / storyteller. I began interviewing awesome presenters around the globe. Taking notes at every event. Learning from masters and from my own big mistakes.

When I became the senior district officer in the largest communications and leadership training organization of the world I was continually asked for tips for success. As a former aircraft mechanic & maintenance specialist my brain thought of everything as a tool. As I visited speaking clubs I would leave them with a Tool For Success. I have assembled over 103 tools, tips and techniques into one location. As I continue to travel the globe I am sure more tools will be found. I will again assemble them into The Speaker's Toolbox #2.

May all of your tools not be a Hammer.
Cheers
Tom

The Speakers Toolbox

Over 103 tools for effective presentations

The Power of the Pause
Tool # 1

Power of the Pause; it draws attention. Pause when you first take the stage, when you pose a question & to emphasize a point. It allows a question to be answered and your audience to reflect.

Converse with Your Audience
Tool # 2

Speak with the intent to have a conversation with the audience. Allow time to react to your statements just as in a 1 to 1 conversation. Encourage a reply to a question.

Incorporate Interruptions
Tool # 3

Include the interruption into your presentation. When a waiter makes an interruption in the room include them as part of what you are trying to emphasize. They will feel included and the audience will wonder if you had staged them as part of the setup.

Reinforce Voice - Stand on your Tiptoes
Tool # 4

Stand on your tiptoes when you speak in a HIGH voice. It will give an illusion of being even higher than normal. Then when you describe looking over a wall or into a window will be very impactful.

Create a Character
Tool # 5

Use a Hat stand to place a hat, it can be another character that you refer to. A strong but silent point of contact on the stage with you.

Test Your Slideware
Tool # 6

Bring your own copy of the PowerPoint, photos or slideshow and make sure it works in the house system 2 hours before your presentation.

Have Your Own Name Badge
Tool # 7

Make and wear your own Name Badge. Use a big font so it is easy to be read. You want all to know who you are, so make it easy for them. Depending on the venue you may want to take it off before going on stage. Be approachable before and after the event.

Carry Safety Pins
Tool # 8

Have five safety pins in your suit jacket, purse or in your resource bag. When you have a costume malfunction you will be glad you had a Safety pin.

"Stage" Your Talk
Tool # 9

Move with purpose on stage. If you have 3 specific points to state, take a step to a new location on stage for each point. Your audience will have a visual emphasis.

Contrast Colors
Tool # 10

Contrasting colors can be seen from the stage. A dark suit needs a solid colored shirt with contrasting color of tie or scarf. Blue suit - white shirt = RED tie. etc.
Wear opposite colors of the back drop. If the hotel provides black curtains and you wear a dark suit you will look like a floating head on stage.

Wear Large Jewelry
Tool # 11

Wear Big Jewelry per Christy Wessler. When you are on stage you need to be 10 – 40% bigger than life. That cute little broach needs to be the size of your hand to be noticed on stage. The same for a man's tie pattern.

"Put Your Hand in Your Pocket"
Tool # 12

From Liz in Denver: I was told to "put my hands in my Pockets!" OK that is not what is normally said but here is WHY. "I was raised Italian / Jewish from New York. I would speak with flagrant arm motions. When I started putting one hand in a pocket, it kept me grounded and then I used only one for gestures and extra emphasis. Yes Put my Hand in my pocket!

Reverse Stage Movement
Tool # 13

Move from right to left for each speaking point. The audience will see it as left to right, the same as they would read a book.

Move, Stop, Speak
Tool # 14

Move on stage to a location. Move with purpose. Stop then speak. Often your words can be lost when you are moving. If you need to be moving when you speak be 15% LOUDER.

Increase Energy for Bigger Audiences
Tool # 15

For every 100 ft. of depth in the audience. Be 10% larger with your animation and arm movements. The bigger the room the bigger the motions. Also be slower.

Point with Your Palm
Tool # 16

Use the Palm of your hand to point to a section of the audience. To point with your index finger is less than polite in many parts of the world.

Brand Your Giveaways
Tool # 17

Have a giveaway for your audience that ties with your branding. Tie it to your most famous Story.

Use Acronyms
Tool # 18

Use acronyms to make your point. Such as I use 3 points to make **H A T H**eart **A**ction **T**rust etc.

Omit Needless Words
Tool # 19

Editing. If a statement doesn't support the theme of your speech or story then eliminate it. Words used for fluff can water down the power of your talk. The Gettysburg Address is only 246 words and is a few minutes long.

Record & Replay Your Talk
Tool # 20

Digital Voice recorders make it easy to practice a talk. It shows the time as you speak than can be easily replayed as you are driving in your car. The sound becomes embedded in your head as you listen to it. Leave it play while you are on the other side of the room doing something else. When your ear hears something strange replay that section. What didn't flow like the rest of the talk?

Wear a Big Watch
Tool # 21

Wear a big watch. Maria said the easiest way for her to keep time was to buy BIG wrist watches that she could casually glance at for time. Yes part of her big jewelry. This works for guys with long sleeves too.

Everyone is Listening but NOT in the Toilet
Tool # 22

Treat every microphone as if it were ON. The moment you assume it is off is when you make a statement that you didn't want the world to hear. Don't wear a cordless microphone to the Restroom! It is too easy to believe it is turned off. If you do have it on, unplug it from the transmitter pack on your belt.

Study Your Body Language
Tool # 23

Watch a video of your performance with the sound off. Do your motions appear to match words? Then play it in fast mode and see how big you get with your arms. It becomes very obvious. Repetitive ticks like pulling your ear, rubbing your hands, scratching your head all show up very clearly.

Dress to Rehearse
Tool # 24

Wear the clothes that you perform in to rehearse in. Not just practice but a true rehearsal. Look at it in a video. Do your shoes support your balance and grounded stance? Do you leave your suit jacket open or closed? Is your tie crooked? Stand in front of different colored backdrops to see how distinctive you can be seen.

Speak to the Cheap Seats
Tool # 25

Speak to the people in the Cheap Seats. Go sit in the cheap seats and have someone else test the sound. When the Cheap Seats can hear you well then everybody can hear you well.

Double Check Your Appearance
Tool # 26

Take one more look in the mirror and also ask someone, anyone, how you look before walking on stage. The unknown shirttail being pulled out, the crooked tie, fly open will be distractive to your presentation.

Secure Your Cables
Tool # 27

Use a twisty tie on your power cords. On your projector tie your computer cable and your power cord together. You need them both and you can't operate if they get separated.

Simplify Recordkeeping
Tool # 28

Staying in a hotel. Charge all incidentals, meals to the room. It is easier to track all expenses. When adding a tip make the total end in $.35. When you check out anything that doesn't have that end will stand out and you can quickly confirm if it was your charge or an incorrect charge to you.

Provide Your Introduction
Tool # 29

Write your own introduction. Make 2 copies to bring with you. Often the one that you sent to your presenter fails to be brought to the event. You can make last minute changes as you meet your audience and see your venue. I like to tell my introducer, "You can say anything you want about me, As long as it is not more than what is on this introduction letter!" It can be difficult to live up to what someone else may say.

Test Audio
Tool # 30

Test the sound system 1 hour before the event. Test your own mikes if you brought them. I was in a convention size hotel in Nashville. The whole sound system had been wired with incorrect polarity so they had adapters for those using their own systems but we didn't know it till we had spent significant time assuming all of our equipment had failed during transport.

No Gum!
Tool # 31

Get rid of the chewing gum. Don't even allow it in your traveling pockets. It can be too easy to pop some in then be on stage. If you see yourself in video (fast forward) chewing gum it will remind you of a cow. Yes less than professional.

Focus on Your Topic
Tool # 32

When you have limited time to present then you have too much information. Edit out the unnecessary words. Take out everything that does not directly apply to your subject. Stick to your subject ONLY. "One way to get air out of a glass is to pour in water". Be Absorbed by Your Subject.

Use a Rug
Tool # 33

Use a Rug! This came from my friend Gail. She is more than sight impaired. She is Blind and a great speaker. She has a small rug placed on the stage where she should be standing & in the direction she should be facing the most. She can feel it with her feet and no one else realizes it. Even other speakers who come to use the stage next rarely notice it.

Scan and Pause
Tool # 34

Scan and pause. Scan the audience as you speak but pause and look at only one person when you make your main phrase or statement. I learned this from Craig Valentine. Now add a call back. Look back to that same person when you refer to that same phrase each time.

Lower Your Voice for Emphasis
Tool # 35

Lower your voice to make an authoritative statement more credible.

Circulate a Sign-in Sheet
Tool # 36

Pass around a sign-in sheet and have them place a check mark by the name if they would like to receive a free email copy of your special report. You build your qualified customer list at each event. They can always opt out with no guilt.

Surprise an Audience Member
Tool # 37

Place a special note under the chair of an audience member for a gift. Use it when the audience has been sitting too long and you need a short physical activity. Have them look under their chair and send the winner to the front of the room.

Greet Your Audience
Tool # 38

Create "interest in the storyteller" by generating a buzz. Greet everyone in the audience as they come in the door, even if it backs them out the door and down the hallway. It makes a powerful personal connection. Just don't make the event late.

Double Duty Business Cards
Tool # 39

Put your tag line on the back of your business card. Use both sides of the card. Double the value of your marketing investment.

Engage All the Senses
Tool # 40

Effective story telling engages the 5 senses. Include taste, touch, smell, sight and sound descriptive words in all parts of your talk, especially the opening and closing. A reminder card of the 5 senses is good. Printed across the top of your presentation Outline is even better.

Use the Whole Stage
Tool # 41

Use the depth of the stage. Come towards the audience to ask a question but lean back or move back when giving them space to answer the question.

Use a Timer
Tool # 42

Keep track of time by using a large LED digital type of clock in the back of the room pointing at you so you can easily see it. Or you can do the opposite and have a small kitchen cooking timer that fits on your lectern or clips to your notes or clipboard. Being on time keeps you professional and the favorite of the event planner.

Use Email to Backup Important Information
Tool # 43

Email yourself a copy of your travel arrangements and event contact person. Also email yourself a copy of the contract. Why? Because you can access your email from anywhere in the world and print off your information. A hardcopy that didn't make it into your briefcase can be reprinted and many unfortunate misunderstandings corrected immediately! You say that you just saved the contract information on your computer. So what do you do if it was your computer that got stolen or broken? Yes go to the internet café and check your email.

Leave Speaking Samples on Your Voicemail
Tool # 44

Call your own voice mail and leave a message. Actually do it 3 different times of the day. It is good to know how you sound when you are being heard over your phone by a potential client. Call & leave a message to yourself early in the morning. Again at noon time. Again in the evening. Do it standing UP and again sitting down. Use a variety of voice ranges. You well soon hear the most pleasing and enthusiastic voice that fits who you want representing YOU. I found for me, when I stand and smile before I make a call my voice projects the best ME. I heard myself leave a message when I was very tired and it was scary!

Use Personal Stories
Tool # 45

Use personal stories to add conviction to your message. "I remember when my dad was teaching me to ride a bike...." Etc.

Limit Filler Words
Tool # 46

Verbal Graffiti! Know how to use it. Toastmasters count the "ums" and "ahs" when you are learning to speak. Other filler words "like you know", "so" are not necessarily bad. There should be enough that you sound human, approachable and conversationally pleasing to hear. Too much of anything is still too much. Have a random person listen and count the "ums" and "ahs" in your presentation and report to you. After years of poor habits these crutch words can creep back in. Do an unbiased test on your speaking skills not just your content every year. An easy way to get an accurate count is to use a hand held tally counter. Give it to an audience member to click every time you use a crutch word unnecessarily. It is better to know than to continue offending the intelligence of others.

Empty Your Pockets
Tool # 47

Empty your pockets of unnecessary stuff. Loose change and keys can become a source of nervous noise. Watch yourself on video and see if you play with your keys in your pocket.

Strategically Place Your Laptop
Tool # 48

When giving a PowerPoint set your laptop on the projector table looking forward. You can then see your own laptop as things are being projected on the screen. You have your own teleprompter! And the audience believes you are looking at them.

Make Use of the Blank Screen Feature
Tool # 49

Have a functional Blank Screen button on your laptop or PowerPoint remote control. So when you walk in front of your projector you can blank the screen and not blind yourself. Often a Storyteller will have a powerful photo to set the tone of the event. You also look far more professional too.

Use Facial Expressions
Tool # 50

Know your FACE. With the common use of the Jumbotron, large screen projectors, it is even more important to understand Facial Gestures. Use them before your Vocal Gestures. Take a Clown workshop. Understanding how your face naturally moves is the first step of applying the accent makeup as a clown. Understanding how easily it is to add an exclamation point to a statement by using your face is POWERFUL. IF you are not being projected on a large screen the effect is almost subliminal. The front of the audience picks up on it and passes the reaction to the members behind them.

Sight Before Sound
Tool # 51

Action before Verbal descriptions engages the audience. When you talk about a giraffe. Start by looking UP to the eyes of the Giraffe and then raising your Down Stage Hand as you begin to describe the size. You will have engaged all of the visual learners in your audience. Those who weren't clear of your description will be through your actions.

Tell Stories Through Dialogue
Tool # 52

Dialogue or Narrations? Do you want your audience to feel as if they are living the story or just reading a book? Using your voice as you are in the conversation engages your audience. John said, "This is the deepest canyon in North America". Or if you said it as John. "If you were with me you could have heard our voices echoing in the deepest canyon in North America."

Eliminate Distracting Bulges
Tool # 53

Eliminate bulges in your Pockets. It is a visual noise. It distracts your audience from your presentation. Take out everything from your pockets. Lock them in your room or travel bag. Keep only what you may need on stage. The items that you need for traveling or shopping you DON'T need on stage.

Prepare a Pre-Show
Tool # 54

Preshow PowerPoint Show for your audience while they are waiting. A series of fun photos that engage and begin to set the premise of our presentation. Let it loop through to entertain and send their thoughts the direction to best receive your message.

Enhance Your Stories
Tool # 55

Be an awesome storyteller with a 6th sense. Add sensory terms to each story. Sight, sound, touch, taste, and the strongest is SMELL. Add the 6th most powerful sense, Humor. Let it be found in your story, avoid forcing it to happen. Listen to how a child will tell a story to hear the questions of what makes sense. Be an awesome storyteller.

WIIFM
Tool # 56

WIIFM In your opening 17 seconds Craft every speech with the number 1 question in the audience's mind as the premise. What's In It for Me, Is truly what everybody is asking in their mind. Be ready to answer WIIFM for any presentation.

Think Like a Hollywood Producer
Tool # 57

Write your presentation like a Hollywood script. Dive in to the action. Expose the characters, have a hero with a goal, uncover the conflict, surpass the conflict and let the resolution be clear. When you are presenting anything, think like a Hollywood Producer and the impact will be powerful for your audience.

Convey Professionalism
Tool # 58

Mindset — be a professional in every way. Professionals are compensated for their communication skills by money, increased business or qualified referrals to your Perfect Client. Have a reminder card or item in your pocket to be a Professional and you will be treated that way.

Provide Mentorship
Tool # 59

Wear a Mentors Hat. Be a mentor to others. They will pose questions to you that you will have to research and learn and then teach to them. Someone in the room aspires to be like you. The Mentor Attitude will keep you vibrant & approachable.

Reveal "Secrets"
Tool # 60

Shh, I have a secret for you. Have a few secrets of your craft to share. Everyone wants to hear a secret. So give them a secret for their success. Make it special and you will have more audience attention.

Backup on the Cloud
Tool # 61

Create an online storage place that you can access from around the world on the internet for free. Store your presentations, contracts, handouts in simple and common file types. From most every hotel you can access them and be saved when your own computer gets that headache of doom.

Incorporate Kinesthetic Mnemonics
Tool # 62

Learn kinesthetic teaching skills. Know how to express your key phrase, your takeaway message using a body action for the audience to eternalize it. The YMCA song is known around the world because people use their full body to form the letter shapes! If your message is "See the Future & remember the Past". You could have people touch their eyes and point forward with their hands. Then touch their head and point to the back with their thumb.

Energize Your Audience
Tool # 63

Have energizing activities every 25 minutes. There are hundreds you can use. Stand up and stretch, move to a new location in the room, interchange with small groups, Print a 6 favorite activities card and keep it in your case to remind you of options.

Bring Adaptors
Tool # 64

Have a multi adaptor for each of your computer, phone, iPad, camera or technology items to charge them. USB chargers are nice and an adapter to a wall outlet is wise. Get 2 and hide 1 in your favorite travel bag that you take on the plane. The times your plane is delayed and you're sitting in the lobby wishing your battery wasn't dead will be far happier.

Pamper your Voice Box
Tool # 65

Take care of your body. Your vocal Folds are one of your major tools. Warm them up and exercise them appropriately. An Olympic marathon runner wouldn't jump into a freezing river after warming up. Their muscles would contract and restrict movement. So will your voice if you drink Cold Water. Have a room temperature class of water available to keep your voice warmed and ready.

Find the Right Remote Control
Tool # 66

Find your favorite electronic pointer to control a computer & PowerPoint program. When it fits your hand, easy to find buttons you will appear magical. Test everyone you see and visit the electronic store often. The one that works for YOU is the one to buy and keep in your travel bag.

Beware of (Some) Beverages
Tool # 67

Drink appropriately. Prior to taking the stage to present be aware of what you drink. Dairy products can coat your throat with a thick film, making it tough to speak and clear your throat. Avoid, milk or chocolates. If you do have some clean your throat with Water with Lemon in it. This gently cleans the throat. Be cautious of Orange juice or other strong acidic drinks. They may clean TOO much. Then you have just the opposite problem!

Carry and Use Breath Fresheners
Tool # 68

Freshening your breath with a small mint can be marvelous. There are many products that we see at every checkout counter. Have some in your travel kit, presenter's bag and in your pocket. Avoid the big container that puts a BULGE in your pocket or Rattles and makes LOTS of unsuspected Noise when you walk! Remember the Seinfeld show when Elaine gave the annoying office worker some to carry. She always knew when he was close!

Carry a Mini-Flashlight
Tool # 69

What do you need when the Lights go out or are dimmed? Or the room monitor just changed the lights for your PowerPoint to be seen and you lose your notes. Or you drop your pen or pointer. You should have a small LED flashlight. Small, easy to have in your pocket. You can use it to find what you dropped plus use it to Signal the sound man in the back or the room. It is much kinder than flashing the Laser Pointer.

Disable Automatic Sleep
Tool # 70

The high-end electronic suppliers make a cool product for keeping your computer from going to hibernation while you are presenting. Too often the computer will try to time out during your presentation! Many high security buildings don't allow some computers to continue to operate without a person actively using it. A cool USB Jiggler keeps the computer active. Check with the security officer at all high security buildings before using it.

Have a Backup Pointer
Tool # 71

Buy 2 PowerPoint pointers. Find the perfect one for you. Test it several times. Than Purchase a second unit. Keep them separate in your travel bags. Mark them with your name & email. The time that it gets left at the last gig will make you very happy you have the 2nd one. The last location will have your name of who to send it to. So you will be in good condition for each gig.

Think Like a Stage Director
Tool # 72

Think like a Stage Director. Before your presentation walk the stage. Identify the best places to be seen, heard and present from. What lighting will make you look the best? Where are you blocking your visual aids? Then using masking tape to Mark Your stage. A simple small X on the stage works well. Now if you have several people using the same stage be aware of which marks are yours! Then just get a roll of price stickers from the office store that are YOUR favorite color. Or have some printed with your NAME and Website for even more marketing.

Internalize Your Message
Tool # 73

Voice recorders are often in you smartphones now. You can practice your talk by recording to your phone. Play it back or transfer it to your computer. While you're driving use a Blue Tooth earpiece. The quality will be better and you can easily rehearse and hear your voice. It will build an internal memory of your words because the Voice is In YOUR head! Practice your Phrase that Pays and listen to yourself saying it until you internalize it.

Carry Two Hotel Key Cards
Tool # 74

Hotel room keys that are credit card magnetic strips can be a headache. They are getting better, however they are easily erased by magnets from name badges, cell phones in the same pocket or even laid too close to some computers! When you check in get 2 keys. Place one in your wallet and the other in the pocket you normally use. You have the spare and won't need to get a new one at 2 am. Bonus, when you know you have a spare you can use it as a joke from the stage. Give your Room Key Away on Stage as a way to cause an unexpected Smile! Give an old room key card from the last hotel to an audience member. Never use the current hotel card, they might get lucky and find your room!

New Socks Make a Big Difference
Tool # 75

Keep your body invigorated. Simple things can make a huge difference. Socks! Wear new socks when on stage. Your feet will be well cushioned and your spine will thank you.

Use Music to Influence Mood
Tool # 76

Music will influence the attitude of your audience. Match the needs of your event. Intro music to increase the energy of anticipation. Upbeat to match your message. During trainings use non vocal music. Increase the volume when in small group sharing's to encourage louder conversation and sharing. Reduce the volume to bring them back to the main group. Royalty Free or Simple paid fee music can be used around the world.

Carry a Translation Dictionary
Tool # 77

Translation dictionary in your travel bag. A small pocket type for the general languages. A few key words are powerful. When you are on stage to give a few words showing how you are willing to learn others languages is a HUGE bonus of integrity. Now with the smartphones you have many choices of APPs that can do this too.

Collect Favorite Quotes
Tool # 78

Have a simple card with several of your favorite quotes. Both serious and funny quotes. Some from your spiritual leader to as funny as Dr. Seuss. When you have them printed as a giveaway you can quickly review them from stage even. It is a Tension Breaker, Time Filler or a Smile Causer when you need it.

Do Voice Exercises
Tool # 79

How do you warm up your voice? The internet has made many apps for smartphones that are marvelous. Find one you like. I have it on my phone with my Bluetooth earpiece engaged. Play it and practice on the way to my gigs. It is fun, simple and works well. It gives me a guide so I don't stress my voice either.

Remind Yourself of Why You Are Speaking
Tool # 80

Carry a Reminder of Why you are on stage? What is your motivator to get out and speak? Is it to empower someone? Motivate because you had been motivated by a mentor? To honor a past close friend? I carry a special toy figure, Mr. Yellow. He reminds me of my best friend and the memories we shared before her passing. I use Mr. Yellow to add even more smiles from the stage because of my best friend Karen & how she affected my life.

Exploit Your Favorite Testimonial
Tool # 81

When someone asks, "Are you any good? Why should I hire you to present for my team?" Give them the perfect referral. Have a copy of your favorite referral easy to find in your Smartphone or laptop. The one that makes you smile and a little embarrassed every time someone reads it out loud. You can show it to potential clients and cinch a good deal with your vulnerability.

Have a Reverent Invocation Ready
Tool # 82

Have a simple prayer, invocation or toast printed and ready. You will be given the opportunity to open a solemn moment. Your ability to have it ready will endear you with huge quantities of respect. Keep the phrase appropriate for the audience. You can always set it up as, "As my dear Grandmother would say…." If it went well great. If it bombed you could say "I never understood why she did things like that."

Carry a Receipt Book
Tool # 83

You will be finishing a presentation, visiting in the room when someone will adamantly want to buy a book you spoke about. Maybe the sample in your hand. Ultimately yes, you will have your own sales forms and marketing goods. You may not have them yet or you do have them but you didn't expect to be selling anything at this particular presentation. Stop by the office supply store and get a generic receipt book that is carbonless. A small one will fit in your bag easily. It can help complete a sale, keep you looking the professional you profess to be and keep your accountant happy.

Always Have a (Clean) Joke Ready
Tool # 84

Have a simple 3 minute joke printed and ready. You will be given the opportunity to add some levity during a meeting. Your ability to have a joke ready will endear you with greatness. Keep it clean and self-effacing humor. A "groaner" of a joke is far better than an off color offensive joke that you can NEVER take back.

Carry "Trivial Pursuit" Cards
Tool # 85

Be ready to add some humor to any event. Stop by a thrift store and buy a used game of Trivial Pursuit. It is OK if it is missing some cards. Take a small handful and stick them in your speaker's toolbox. When you have extra moments in a presentation that are tense or you need to stall for time, pull out a few cards and turn it in to a prize winning game. You can include the audience as the host while you run to fix the projector or get a needed document, etc.

Balance Group Energy
Tool # 86

To diffuse the energy of a group. Like at a conference where they have just been given many awards and the bragging is HIGH, invite several recipients to the front of the room. Let them get it out. So you can re-ground them. Get them humble again to start learning what you are teaching them. Let them know how much more they can grow from here.

Create a Mock-up of an Unfinished Book
Tool # 87

Have a mockup of your soon-to-be-published book to show. A simple color print out of the cover can be powerful. Make a cover and wrap it around another book that you love and believe it is yours till yours is published. Whip it out and read a few quotes. It is powerful how much people will attach the words you are reading to the YOU that they are seeing.

Capture Testimonials on Your Smartphone
Tool # 88

Establish credibility by using someone else as your expert. Testimonials in writing are good, in audio are great & on Video are powerful. Using a Smartphone can capture very real testimonials that can be on your blog or website. Keep a 14 year old kid around to run your Smartphone or at the least to train you how to make short videos.

Carry Your Two Favorite Mentors' Books
Tool # 89

Have a copy of 2 books who have mentored you to your success, both serious and funny books. Something from your spiritual leader to as funny as a bedtime story book. Showing your vulnerability is an emotional connector that lasts. I have Dale Carnegie, How to Win Friends.. and a Dr. Seuss book. It is a Tension Breaker, Time Filler or a Smile Causer when you need it.

Take Improv Classes
Tool # 90

Improv classes will build skills in confidence that are awesome. The ability and willingness to deal with anything on stage will be worth the time to take an improv class. When you have taken a few classes there will be some powerful phrases that you can use over and over again. Have them printed on small reminder cards and placed in your presenter's bag. Refresh your mind of them before you begin. Some of my favorite are, "Yes and …", "Show, don't Tell" & "Know, you can't say NO". These both will keep the flow of a presentation moving forward and engaging.

Use Three & Seven
Tool # 91

Odd numbers are funny and catch the attention of the audience. The numbers 3 & 7 are key in comedy. When you announce the price of something have it end on an odd amount. 703 gallons of lemon juice will have anyone pucker up! If I had 7 fingers I could change a baby's diaper faster. If you have 3 twins, would it be 6 or a pair and a half = 3? You can do this with your marketing and pricing too. Have your least expensive item at $97 then to up to $297, $497, $997 to $2497.

Encourage Equal Participation
Tool # 92

How do you get more people to share during a training? There often are 1 or 2 people always wanting to answer or engage from the audience. So you can get a wider participation by having a few different phrases to encourage greater participation. "Let's hear from others we have not heard form yet." "Who else agrees with her statement? Why?", "Who could rephrase that so I can say it to my grandmother?"

Offer Incentives
Tool # 93

Offer incentives for taking a risk. During your trainings if you ask someone to respond and it is a bit risky for them. Give them a Reward or a gift. Maybe your book, a toy, a memorable item to take back home or to their office. They will have to explain all about it to everyone they meet. Make it cool and memorable of YOUR brand.

Collect Magazine Covers
Tool # 94

Watch for outrageous Magazine covers at the grocery store checkout stand. The more you say, "I can't believe someone wasted ink to print this" the better it is. Why? You want to have this outrageous item to pull out when the TENSION gets too high during presentation. You want to bring the audience back to reality. Let them know you are human and see how un-serious life should be. When you have the actual magazine it adds validity.

Keep a Pre-Packed Speaking Case
Tool # 95

Your Traveling Toolbox, your mobile office with your books, products, order forms, etc. should not be the shiniest item around. Yes, it is part of your presentation and appearance. The danger of it being TOO nice is how things get stolen. Diamond Brokers don't carry a beautiful case with a label that says "Expensive Items Inside". A punk thief will take what looks expensive first. It is OK to appear a little worn. Still in good secure condition but not looking like a bag of diamonds.

Carry Spare Batteries
Tool # 96

Have two spare batteries for every electronic item you carry. It is during your event that the battery will die. Not at the end. Not during your setup. It is Murphy's Law that it happens when it is least convenient! And the one electronic item that has the special size of battery is the one that fails when there is no store within three hours of your location. Keep them in a heavy zip lock bag so their contacts can't drain the power out of them or leak on your clothes either.

Bring a "Toolbox"
Tool # 97

What are you physically taking to your presentations? How do you carry your notes, sign-in sheets, books to sell, etc.? We are referring to a toolbox throughout this book. When I talk and present a class for Presenters I do bring in an actual Metal Toolbox. It is a visual anchor for the workshop. What I take to a gig at a Rotary or service club, a keynote in a hotel, a 3 day training is different. I use 2 different types of luggage carriers. For local gigs it is a roll around case that holds my table cloth, table top display frame, books, CD's, order forms, pins, credit card swiper, safety pins, etc. (most every item listed in this book in appropriate quantities). When I am traveling on a Plane I use a full roll around suit case that still fits in the overhead compartment. Everything I may need to operate my business when 200 miles away from my office. Be sure it doesn't get too heavy. You should have spare products and extra items in your checked baggage. When 1 bag gets lost you still have a chance to operate and have a successful gig.

Generate Buzz with Social Media
Tool # 98

Social media updater system will get your current event out simply and quickly to all of your internet connections. Facebook, LinkedIn, Twitter and then the newest sites available too. Post it once and then share the fun with everyone else You can encourage your audience to update just before you take a break in your presentation. It can be a viral marketing opportunity.

www.TheSpeakersToolbox**BOOK**.com

Carry Painters' Tape
Tool # 99

Travelers roll of painters masking tape. The good stuff that will come off without taking the paint off of the wall. Most hotels will not allow you to tape a sign to a wall if there is any chance it may damage the surface. The Blue Painters Masking tape is designed to protect the wall and is acceptable by most hotels.

Create a Hero
Tool # 100

Make someone a hero and you will be elevated. Before your gig or while you are setting up find a hero in the room. Find someone who has done something well and brag about it. When you honor others they quickly elevate you in return. Be sincere in your praise. It can be as simple as seeing someone hold the door for others or a big recognition they received. You can enhance their reward by a gift from you like your book or CD product. This is "paying it forward" marketing that works well.

Step into Character
Tool # 101

When speaking as 2 or more characters, take a physical step into the direction of the character speaking. It will be far more distinctive between the two.

Save Your Name Badges
Tool # 102

Save a few name badges from your events. The lanyard type and the clip-on type. Keep them in your bag to use. Place your own business card in it when YOU need to be known. You can modify many of the clips to fit the badge you get at a conference that is the safety pin type. I am at so many events that using the safety pins ultimately damages my clothes. A clip on is far kinder.

Pull Emotions from Memory
Tool # 103

Smile from a childhood memory. It will come from the heart. Use your eyes when you smile and the feeling can be felt in the back of an auditorium.

Insert Your Business Card into Your Book
Tool # 104

Be remembered after a book sell. Place your business card, personalized bookmark or post card into every book you sell. During printing they can blow the card into the pages before shipping or you can sit and stuff one in while you are sitting by the hotel pool.

Resources

Here are a few of the professionals who have influenced and mentored me:

Joe Sabah	JoeSabah.com
Darren LaCroix	DarrenLacroix.com
Ed Tate	EdTate.com
Rich Hopkins	RichHopkins.com
Joan Janis	JoanJanis.com
Terri Larsen	ProfLarsen.com
Bob Proctor	http://www.proctorgallagherinstitute.com/
Brian Tracy	BrianTracy.com
Steve Siebold	SteveSiebold.com
Christy Wessler	http://www.bighaired.com
Craig Valentine	CraigValentine.com

To see reviews of this book and other Awesome Speaker Products go to:

Awesome**Speaker**Products.com

Index

You can order more copies, both digital and hardcopy by going to

www.TheSpeakersToolbox**BOOK**.com

Also by Tom Hobbs:

Be The Master of Ceremonies not the Amateur of Events CD and MP3 can be purchased at
TheManInTheHat.net

Tom & his team are eager to help you & your organization Increase Profits by Causing more Smiles

You can learn more about Powerful Branding, Causing Smiles and The Man in the Hat by visiting TheManInTheHat.net

Order more copies of this book by using this QR

www.TheSpeakersToolbox**BOOK**.com

Made in the USA
Lexington, KY
11 May 2017